THIS BOOK BELONGS TO:

_____

The Wonderful World of God

Mimi Jones

Dedicated to all the believers.

All rights reserved.
No part of this book may be reproduced in any form or by any means, electronic or mechanical, and no photocopying or recording, unless you have written permission from the author.

ISBN 978-1-958985-36-6

Copyright © 2025 by Mimi Jones

www.joeysavestheday.com

A Mimi Book

WELCOME TO THE WONDERFUL WORLD OF GOD

DARKNESS

LIGHT

Day 1

God said, Let the waters bring forth abundantly the moving creature that hath life, and fowl that may fly above the earth in the open firmament of heaven.

Genesis 1:20

Living Creatures

Day 6

Male/Female

God rests.

The Lord said unto Noah, Come thou and all thy house into the ark; for thee have I seen righteous before me in this generation.

Genesis 7:1

Noah's Ark

Moses parts the Red Sea

But lift thou up thy rod, and stretch out thine hand over the sea, and divide it, and the children of Israel shall go on dry ground through the midst of the sea.

Exodus 14:16

The Ten Commandments

You shall have no other gods before me.
You shall not make for yourself an idol.
You shall not misuse the name of the Lord your God.
Remember the Sabbath day by keeping it holy.
Honor your father and your mother.
You shall not murder.
You shall not commit adultery.
You shall not steal.
You shall not give false testimony against your neighbor.
You shall not covet.

Exodus 20:1-17

BELIEVE

For God so loved the world, that he gave his only begotten Son, that whosoever believeth in him should not perish, but have everlasting life.

John 3:16

Now, the birth of Jesus Christ was on this wise, When his mother Mary was espoused to Joseph before they came together, she was found with a child of the Holy Ghost.

Matthew 1:18

For I came down from heaven, not to do mine own will, but the will of him that sent me.

John 6:38

THE LORD IS MY

Light

AND

Salvation

GOD
BLESS
YOU

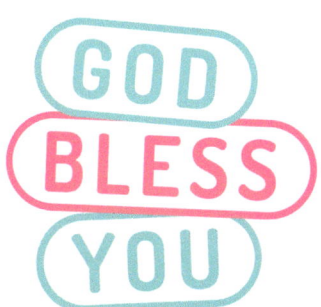

PSALM 27:1

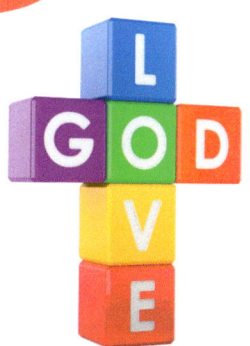

www.ingramcontent.com/pod-product-compliance
Lightning Source LLC
Chambersburg PA
CBHW040028050426
42453CB00002B/47